BIG HEARTS

 SEEDS OF FAITH

Hi, my name is **Tino**! I have been practicing karate and my dance moves for a while now, and I'm getting pretty good. I love my twin brother, Sebastian, even though we're different—I'm older, but he's taller!

Hello! My name is **Sebastian**. I have a twin brother, Tino, and a baby sister named Aly. Science is kind of my thing. I love working on experiments with my best friend, Lily, and when I grow up I want to be a scientist!

Hello, my name is **Pia**! It's just my mom, dad, and me in our family. I love playing the violin and spending time with my best friend, Amani. I can speak two languages and want to learn more!

Hey, I'm **Liam**! I'm pretty good at sports and I love to bake. One time I won a ribbon in a cake competition! I love doing things with my family, especially my siblings, Sarah and Owen, and my dog, Pepper.

Big Hearts, Seeds of Faith
© 2021 by Pam Bowers and Kim Bowers

Written by Pam and Kim Bowers
Illustrated by Nadia Ronquillo

Published in La Vergne, Tennessee by Ingramspark

Cataloging-in-Publication Data has been applied for and may be should be obtained from the Library of Congress.

ISBN: 978-0-578-86223-1

Printed in USA

Mfr: DSC / LaVergne, TN USA / May 2021

How to Read this Book

Parents, Families, and Caregivers,

We designed this book to be a tool to help you topically address and maneuver through current daily struggles in your child's life. Different from many of its counterparts, this book does not have a narrative story, but rather is meant to be a platform for conversation between you and your child. It can be used both retrospectively and proactively to help your child build strong character. Additionally, because of the non-narrative style, you can skip around the book in any order as your child needs...you don't need to read it cover to cover! Pick a scenario as the need arises and discuss them one at a time.

The pictures are the driving force of your conversation—feel free to examine every inch of them! Every two pages focus on a single scenario. We suggest you start with the image on the left as it initiates the scenario, showing the character as they wrestle with navigating challenging situations. Then, examine the page on the right. This side revisits the scenario introduced on the left, but shows the character successfully navigating their big emotions in such a way that helps develop a big heart and strong character. Each image also comes with a series of questions on a sticky note, which serve as a starting guide to help you and your child talk about what you see in each image, the difference in the characters' reactions, and how your child reacts similarly or differently. As you both get comfortable with this inviting learning and sharing style, you will find it easy to eventually think of your own questions to emphasize other characteristics you'd like to work on.

Start with the guiding questions to begin conversations around emotions and responses, and then move to the practical section (the big paragraph on the right page) to enhance your discussion. Each practical section includes various combinations of validation (e.g., "Wanting to win is a good thing"), normalization (e.g.,"Sharing with other people is not always the first thing that we want to do"), and coping strategies (e.g., "When this happens, we need to stop in the moment, take a second to pause, and shift the way that we're thinking.") to help you as caregivers open the lines of communication with your child and help lay a foundation for their faith. These practical sections can also serve as models for you to create your own discussions with your child. Finally, finish with the scripture and prayer. Revisiting these scenarios often can help your child grasp these concepts and apply them as life happens.

The general structure of the book and practical sections come from our collective experiences as a mother/world-ranked coach and a former educator/PhD student. We have found that using this structure and these strategies have been helpful for the children we interact with. As fellow friends, caregivers, and educators, we hope aspects of our model will be helpful for you and yours. Although what we give to you in this book comes from our own personal experiences, we have come to know that scholarly research shares many commonalities. References are available on our website at www.smoothsailingbooks.com.

We wish you all the best! The journey that comes with raising children is not always smooth sailing, but is one that is worth the effort.

Your Friends,

Pam & Kim

Table of Contents

8 Living Joyfully

8 Finding Happiness in the Small Things

10 Rejoicing with Others

12 Developing Awareness of Surroundings

14 Having Compassion

14 When Someone is Hurt

16 For the Poor

18 When Someone is Sad

20 Being Thoughtful

20 When Someone is Sick

22 Helping Around the House

24 Playing with Others

26 Fostering Gratitude

26 When You Get Something You Don't Want

28 When You Don't Get Anything

30 Contentment

32 Giving Respect

32 Talking Back to Parents

34 Talking Bad About Teachers

36 Respecting Your Things

38 Saying "Please and Thank You"

40 Sharing Generously

40 Sharing Our Things

42 Giving Our Time

Living Joyfully

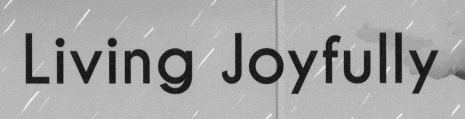

But we were gonna go to the park!

Welp, there go my plans for today.

Discussion Questions

For this page

1. What do you think is happening in the picture?
2. How is Amani feeling?
3. What might she be thinking? What about her face and body show you this?
4. What is Amani doing because of her feelings?
5. How do your face and body look when you feel these things?
6. What do you do when you feel this way?

For that page

7. Revisit questions 1-6 with the other image.
8. What is different about Amani's reaction here than in the other picture?

8

When our plans don't happen the way we want them to, we can feel disappointed, sad, or even angry. We may even try to find a way to get what we want or pout because of our feelings. It's okay to feel those things—not getting what we want is hard! As we recognize these feelings, it is also important to know that we cannot let them boss us around. It is good to stop in the moment, pause, and shift the way that we're thinking. God calls us to be thankful in all situations. So, talk about how you feel and then look for things to be joyful about, like the fun things you get to do instead. Sometimes, a change in plans can bring great surprises!

1 Thessalonians 5: 16-18 (NIV) "Be joyful always; pray continually; give thanks in all circumstances, for this is God's will for you in Christ Jesus."

I guess today is going to be a better day to build our fort!!

I call dibs on the tower!

If we put the blanket at this angle, the weight should make it hold itself up!

Pray- "Dear Father God, thank you for the awesome surprises you gave me today. I pray that you will help my heart be happy when plans change. Please help me have eyes that look for the good things and not eyes that focus on the bad. In Jesus' name I pray, Amen."

There will be many times in your life when you will not be the winner, the favorite, the best, or chosen first. Wanting to win is a good thing; however, we cannot let our desire to win take away our joy for other people. God desires for us to be humble winners and gracious losers.

You did a **great job, Sam!**

Seeing everyone else so happy is making me happy, too!

God is always proud of you and is your biggest fan! Knowing that he is always cheering us on allows us to be able to be joyful for other people when God decides that it's their turn.

Proverbs 3:27 (NIV) "Do not withhold good from those who deserve it, when it is in your power to act."

Pray- *"Dear Father God, thank you for giving me turns to be the winner and for helping me when I am not the winner. I love knowing that you are always cheering me on and are proud of me. Please help me to be joyful for other people. In Jesus' name I pray, Amen."*

11

Discussion Questions
For this page
1. What do you think is happening in the picture?
2. How is Tino feeling?
3. What might he be thinking? What about his face and body show you this?
4. What is Tino doing because of his feelings?
5. How do your face and body look when you feel these things?
6. What do you do when you feel this way?
For that page
7. Revisit questions 1-6 with the other image.
8. What is different about Tino's reaction here than in the other picture?

When we are excited, it is easy to forget where we are and what is going on around us. Our joy overflows and all we focus on are the things we are excited about! We might be too excited to walk with our parents, or we may even start talking loudly. While it is good to be excited and happy for the things we get to do or receive, we also need to be aware of what is going on around us. This helps us to be safe and respectful of where we are. God wants us to be wise and thoughtful for how we live so that we can fully enjoy the things that make our hearts happy!

Thanks for holding my hand and walking with us.

If you bounce high enough, it feels like you're flying!

First, I want to go on the bouncy slide!

I'll be right behind you!

Then, I'm going to climb through the obstacle course!

Ephesians 5:15 (MSG) "So watch your step. Use your head. Make the most of every chance you get."

Pray- "Dear Father God, thank you for all of the fun things you have planned for me to do. Please help me not to get carried away in my excitement, but to remember the rules of where I am so that I can enjoy the fun to the fullest! In Jesus' name I pray, Amen."

13

Having Compassion

Discussion Questions

For this page

1. What do you think is happening in the picture?
2. How is Noah feeling?
3. What might he be thinking? What about his face and body show you this?
4. What is Noah doing because of his feelings?
5. How do your face and body look when you feel this way?
6. What do you do when you feel this way?

For that page

7. Revisit questions 1-6 with the other image.
8. What is different about Noah's reaction here than in the other picture?

14

Helping other people when they are hurt might not be the first thing we want to do. We might have to pause our game, turn off a show, or stop what we are doing to help them. When we don't want to do these things, we need to think about how we would feel if no one came to help us when we are hurt. Jesus stopped what he was doing whenever sick or hurting people came to him. God wants us to care for each other as we would hope others would care for us.

Colossians 3:12 (CSB) "Therefore as God's chosen ones, holy and dearly loved, put on compassion, kindness, humility, gentleness, and patience."

Pray- "Dear Father God, thank you for all of the ways that you, my friends, and my family are here to help me when I am hurt. Please help me to care for others when they are hurting. In Jesus' name I pray, Amen."

Discussion Questions

For this page

1. What do you think is happening in the picture?
2. How is Pia feeling?
3. What might she be thinking? What about her face and body show you this?
4. What is Pia doing because of her feelings?
5. How do your face and body look when you feel this way?
6. What do you do when you feel this way?

For that page

7. Revisit questions 1-6 with the other image.
8. What is different about Pia's reaction here than in the other picture?

16

As you go about your day, you may meet people who do not have the same things you have. Maybe you're at school and another student doesn't have as nice shoes or you're out with your parents and a person asks them if they have any money they can share. Your first thought might not be a desire to get to know these people. At the same time, we must remember that we are all God's children! God calls us to love our neighbors as he loves us, and he wants to use us to show his love. A great place to start is volunteering to serve others or donating our things. What other ways can you think of?

John 15:12 (NIV) "This is my command: Love one another the way I have loved you. This is the very best way to love."

Pray- "Dear Father God, thank you for all of the amazing things you have given me: my family, my home, my toys, my church, and my school. Please help me to pay attention to the people around me so that I can love them the way you love me. In Jesus' name I pray, Amen."

Has there ever been a time when you felt sad, lonely, or upset? Our friends and family feel these same things, too. When others tell us how they are feeling, we might not know what to say or do and that's okay! One thing we can always do is listen. You can even ask the person what they need that would help them feel better. It is important that we do this because God is there for us when we feel the same way. You never know how much better you might make another person feel just by being there for them!

Group hug!!!

I'm so sad. My fishy died and I miss her!

I'm sorry. Do you want a hug?

2 Corinthians 1:4a (NLT) "He comforts us in all our troubles so that we can comfort others..."

Pray- "Dear Father God, thank you for wanting to use me to care for the people around me. Help me to be there for others when they are sad and to remind them of how much you love them. In Jesus' name I pray, Amen."

Being Thoughtful

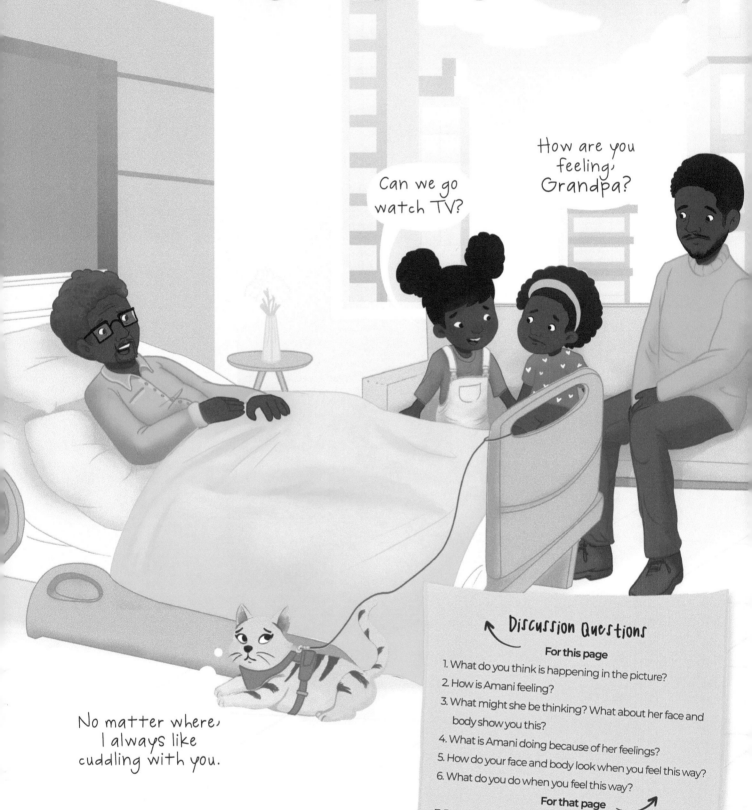

Helping others is like a scavenger hunt: There are many hidden opportunities that we'll find if we take the time to look! These opportunities can be big, like visiting people who are not feeling well, or small, like letting someone go ahead of you in line for the drinking fountain. But like a scavenger hunt, if we aren't searching for ways to help, then we will overlook them. When we think about what others need or like, we are thinking the same way that Jesus did! Jesus knew that the joy that comes from thinking of others is often better than the joy that comes from thinking only about ourselves.

Acts 20:35b (NIV) "Remembering the words that the Lord Jesus himself said: It is more blessed to give than to receive."

Pray- *"Dear Father God, thank you for giving me the fun scavenger hunt of thinking of others. Help me to see all the opportunities you have hidden for me to find. In Jesus' name I pray, Amen."*

Discussion Questions

For this page

1. What do you think is happening in the picture?
2. How is Liam feeling?
3. What might he be thinking? What about his face and body show you this?
4. What is Liam doing because of his feelings?
5. How do your face and body look when you feel this way?
6. What do you do when you feel this way?

For that page

7. Revisit questions 1-6 with the other image.
8. What is different about Liam's reaction here than in the other picture?

22

Cleaning the house, doing chores, and other responsibilities are far less fun than playing outside or watching a movie. It's wild to think, but as much as you dislike chores, so do your parents! But, your parents love you so much that they are willing to set aside the things they enjoy doing to think of your family's needs. This isn't something that they necessarily have to do, but choose to do because they love God and they love you. What can you do to show that same care and love? Picking up toys, clearing the table after you eat, and dusting around the house are great ways that you can be thoughtful to your family.

Can you help me clean the house by picking up your toys before you head outside?

Sure, Mom!

Whoever picks up the most toys is the winner!

I can help, too!

Hebrews 10:24 (ESV) "And let us consider how to stir up one another to love and good works."

Pray- "Dear Father God, thank you for all the ways my family takes care of me, especially when they do the not-so-fun things! Help me to see their thoughtfulness and to find ways to think of them, too. In Jesus' name I pray, Amen."

23

24

Have you ever wanted to do something only to have a friend tell you no? How did you feel? Have you ever felt so excited when someone is happy to do what you want to do? Each one of us has our own likes and dislikes. We have the choice to either encourage others and honor God or do things our way. If we go around only thinking about what we want, we may hurt the people around us—they may even end up playing with others because they don't feel considered! Thinking of what others like and dislike is one way that God tells us to let them know that we care about them.

Hebrews 13:16 (NIV) "And do not forget to do good and to share with others, for with such sacrifices God is pleased."

Pray- *"Dear Father God, thank you for making each of us with different likes and dislikes. Please help me learn to think of others, too, and not just myself. In Jesus' name I pray, Amen."*

Big or small, expensive or cheap, gifts are very special! Not only are they special because someone decided to do something for you, but they are also special because someone saw something and thought of you! Having people think of us in this way is one way that they show that they care about us. So when you get a gift, remembering the time and energy that was put into each gift will help your heart be grateful—even if it's not your favorite thing! Having a grateful heart encourages the gift-giver and makes God happy.

Thanks! I'll definitely have to learn ballet now.

I Thessalonians 5:18 (ICB) "Give thanks whatever happens. That is what God wants for you in Christ Jesus."

Pray- "Dear Father God, thank you for all of the gifts (big and small) that I have been given. Please help me to remember all the effort that was put into the gift so that I can be grateful even when I'm given something I don't want. In Jesus' name I pray, Amen."

Discussion Questions

For this page

1. What do you think is happening in the picture?
2. How is Tino feeling?
3. What might he be thinking? What about his face and body show you this?
4. What is Tino doing because of his feelings?
5. How do your face and body look when you feel this way?
6. What do you do when you feel this way?

For that page

7. Revisit questions 1-6 with the other image.
8. What is different about Tino's reaction here than in the other picture?

Watching someone else get something when you don't get anything can make you feel left out, not thought of, jealous, or even that things are unfair. It's okay to feel those things. Everyone feels this way at different times! Sometimes, you will be the one who gets the toy or is picked to do something. Other times, you will not. In life, we cannot always control these things, but we can control our attitudes. God wants us to be happy for other people because he is doing things to encourage them, just like he does for us! When people we know and love get things or are picked to do something, let's be grateful that God loves those that we love, too.

Romans 12:15a (NIV) "Rejoice with those who rejoice"

Pray- *"Dear Father God, thank you that we all can have special friends. Sometimes it hurts my feelings when others get things and I don't. Please help me learn to be happy for others and not be so focused on myself. In Jesus' name I pray, Amen."*

Discussion Questions

For this page

1. What do you think is happening in the picture?
2. How is Pia feeling?
3. What might she be thinking? What about her face and body show you this?
4. What is Pia doing because of her feelings?
5. How do your face and body look when you feel this way?
6. What do you do when you feel this way?

For that page

7. Revisit questions 1-6 with the other image.
8. What is different about Pia's reaction here than in the other picture?

Practicing gratitude is not always easy, especially when a friend or your siblings get something new. Being grateful for the things that you already have is called contentment. It's okay to want new things, but we can get ourselves into sticky situations when we are not happy with what we have because we will always be wanting something new! If we are content, however, we find reasons to always be happy because we see the many blessings that God has already given us! What are you grateful for?

Proverbs 14:30 (CEV) "It's healthy to be content, but envy can eat you up."

Pray- "Dear Father God, thank you for all your many gifts to me; big and small, old and new. Please help me be happy with what I have, as well as happy for others and all that they have. In Jesus' name I pray, Amen."

Giving Respect

Amani, can you feed Pudge?

No, that's Jada's job!

I could eat a whale!

PUDGE

Discussion Questions

For this page

1. What do you think is happening in the picture?
2. How is Amani feeling?
3. What might she be thinking? What about her face and body show you this?
4. What is Amani doing because of her feelings?
5. How do your face and body look when you feel this way?
6. What do you do when you feel this way?

For that page

7. RRevisit questions 1-6 with the other image.
8. What is different about Amani's reaction here than in the other picture?

Being asked to do something that you don't want to do is not fun. When this happens, you might want to complain, talk back, or ignore what you're being asked to do. Everyone has felt these things at some point and has been tempted to react in one of those ways! We need to understand, though, that if we act in one of those ways, we are being disrespectful and unkind to the person who is asking for our help. God calls us to respect other people, and we show that by listening, speaking kindly, and following directions quickly.

1 Peter 2:17 (ICB) "Show respect for all people. Love the brothers and sisters of God's family. Respect God. Honor the king."

Amani, can you feed Pudge?

Okay, Dad!

Yummy, yummy!

Get in my tummy!

Pray- *"Dear Father God, thank you for putting people in my life. Please help me to give them the respect you call me to give them. Help me to listen, speak kindly, and follow directions quickly with a happy heart. In Jesus' name I pray, Amen."*

PUDGE

Sounds like you're the meanest.

Ugh! That's Mr. Stewart

I don't like him.

He's the meanest!

Discussion Questions

For this page

1. What do you think is happening in the picture?
2. How is Liam feeling?
3. What might he be thinking? What about his face and body show you this?
4. What is Liam doing because of his feelings?
5. How do your face and body look when you feel this way?
6. What do you do when you feel this way?

For that page

7. Revisit questions 1-6 with the other image.
8. What is different about Liam's reaction here than in the other picture?

People will not always be kind towards us—adults included. We cannot control the actions of others, but we can choose how we react to them. When an adult treats us in ways that hurt our feelings, we might want to stop listening or say mean things about them when they are not there. While these reactions may make us feel better, these kinds of choices do not honor God. If you have the chance to tell the adult how you feel, always do. However, if you can't do this or if it doesn't help them change, then you still do not have the excuse to treat them unkindly—although you should seek help from another adult or family member. Jesus tells us to go above and beyond to love our enemies, no matter how they treat us.

Proverbs 21:23 (ICB) "A person who is careful about what he says keeps himself out of trouble."

If you don't have anything nice to chirp, then don't chirp at all!

Hello, Liam!

Hi, Mr. Stewart!

Pray- "Dear Father God, thank you for giving me Jesus and his example for how to treat others. When others do not treat me kindly, please help me to still treat them with respect and kindness. In Jesus' name I pray, Amen."

Discussion Questions
For this page
1. What do you think is happening in the picture?
2. How is Lily feeling?
3. What might she be thinking? What about her face and body show you this?
4. What is Lily doing because of her feelings?
5. How do your face and body look when you feel this way?
6. What do you do when you feel this way?
For that page
7. Revisit questions 1-6 with the other image.
8. What is different about Lily's reaction here than in the other picture?

36

When we first get something, we find ourselves taking good care of it. If it's a pair of shoes, we try not to get a scuff on them. If it's a tablet, we make sure to set it down nicely so we don't break it. But, as time goes on and our new thing becomes old, we might not do as much to take care of it. God tells us to take care of our things because they are really his! When we realize that these things really belong to God, it makes us want to treat them with respect. No one wants to let someone borrow something only to get it back broken!

Please put your tablet away!

Time to go, Lily.

I wish you carried me as gently as you do your tablet!

Okay!

James 1:17 (NIV) "Every good and perfect gift is from above, coming down from the Father of the heavenly lights, who does not change like shifting shadows."

Pray- *"Dear Father God, thank you for all of the many cool things I have. Please help me remember that they belong to you so that I will take better care of them. In Jesus' name I pray, Amen."*

38

When you show respect, it is important to think of what you're saying and how you're saying it. Using words like "please" and "thank you" are not only kind but also respectful. Looking people in the eyes and speaking in a kind tone of voice are also important. When we are in a rush, very excited, extra hungry, or feeling impatient, it's harder to show people respect. God desires us to show everyone respect all the time. But how? Taking a minute to slow yourself down and thinking of how your actions make others feel will help make putting these things into practice a little easier.

Proverbs 16:24 (ICB) "Pleasant words are like a honeycomb. They make a person happy and healthy."

Pray- *"Dear Father God, thank you for all the things I get to do and all the people that help me along the way. When I talk, please help me to remember that what I say and how I say it are important parts of showing respect. In Jesus' name I pray, Amen."*

Sharing Generously

It looks like you're not even using it, Sebastian.

Ummm... No. It's mine and I need it.

Hey Sebastian, can I borrow that pillow?

I need it to practice my karate!

Discussion Questions

For this page

1. What do you think is happening in the picture?
2. How is Sebastian feeling?
3. What might he be thinking? What about his face and body show you this?
4. What is Sebastian doing because of his feelings?
5. How do your face and body look when you feel this way?
6. What do you do when you feel this way?

For that page

7. Revisit questions 1-6 with the other image.
8. What is different about Sebastian's reaction here than in the other picture?

You can borrow mine, too!

Sharing with other people is not always the first thing that we want to do. Sometimes we don't want to share because we don't know if it will be given back to us, or if the other person will take care of it. While we can't control these things, we shouldn't let it stop us from sharing our things with others. When God blesses us with things, he doesn't share them with us just for us to keep them for ourselves! He shares them with us with the desire that we share them with others!

Hey Sebastian, can I borrow that pillow?

I need it to practice my karate!

Sure, Tino! Just bring it back to me when you're done.

Matthew 5:42 (NIV) *"Give to the one who asks you, and do not turn away from the one who wants to borrow from you."*

Pray- *"Dear Father God, thank you for sharing so generously with me. I pray that I remember this whenever someone asks me to share with them. Please help my heart to give as happily as yours when you give to me. In Jesus' name I pray, Amen."*

Discussion Questions

For this page

1. What do you think is happening in the picture?
2. How is Pia feeling?
3. What might she be thinking? What about her face and body show you this?
4. What is Pia doing because of her feelings?
5. How do your face and body look when you feel this way?
6. What do you do when you feel this way?

For that page

7. Revisit questions 1-6 with the other image.
8. What is different about Pia's reaction here than in the other picture?

Sharing isn't just about being generous with your things; sharing includes being generous with your time! No matter how old you are, time is one thing that you can always give. It's easy to spend time with friends and do things you like, but sometimes when you're around new people or maybe doing things you don't enjoy it can feel difficult. When we give our time to encourage or help others, we care for them and show them that they are important. They are usually happier because of the time we spent with them and our hearts feel the joy that comes from sharing our time with others. Let's spend time with all kinds of people not to make ourselves happy but to make them happy!

Luke 6:33a (NIV) "If you do good to those who do good to you, what credit is that to you?"

Pray- *"Dear Father God, thank you for showing me what it means to give generously through Jesus. I pray that I can give my time to others with the same heart as Jesus when he gave to the sick and the hurting. In Jesus' name I pray, Amen."*

Big Hearts, Seeds of Faith

Written by Pam and Kim Bowers
Illustrated by Nadia Ronquillo

About the Authors:

Pam and Kim Bowers are a mother-daughter writing team. Pam is a World Top 50 Master Junior Golf Instructor with a passion for child character development. Kim holds a degree in Psychology and an M.Ed. in Curriculum and Instruction, Elementary Education. She is also a doctoral student for School Psychology.

Together, they share a rich history of growing in Christ as disciples, servant leaders in His kingdom, and best friends. Their life experiences, trials and errors, and God-given talents lend a unique and practical perspective in creating tools to help support God's children and their parents/caregivers.

Smooth Sailing Co.

Visit us at www.smoothsailingbooks.com and @smoothsailingbooks on Instagram.

About the Illustrator:

Nadia Ronquillo is a children's book illustrator, visual development artist and content creator from Ecuador. After receiving her Bachelor's in Graphic Design and Audiovisual Production, she started freelancing as a children's book illustrator and collaborating remotely as a visual development artist with studios in Latin America. She is now developing a tv series show for kids.

For more, visit www.nadiaronquilloart.com and @nadiaronquilloart on Instagram.

Lightning Source UK Ltd.
Milton Keynes UK
UKHW050318311222
414666UK00012B/58